THE THAMES

A Pictorial Journey

THE THAMES

A Pictorial Journey

RICHARD BAIN

Foreword by
LLOYD ROBERTSON

National Library of Canada Cataloguing in Publication

Bain, Richard (Richard G.), 1954-
The Thames: A Pictorial Journey / Richard Bain.

ISBN 0-9687083-5-8

1. Thames River (Ont.)--Pictorial works. I. Title.

FC3095.T415B33 2003   971.3'2'00222   C2003-900642-5
F1059.T415B33 2003

07   06   05   04   03   1   2   3   4   5

Copyright © 2003 by Richard Bain
Tel: 519.660.6424
e-mail: richardbain@bellnet.ca

Published and Distributed by
BINEA PRESS
e-mail: binea@canada.com

Design by Susan Williams
Brian Williams & Associates
Tel: 519.657.1529
e-mail: swilliams@on.aibn.com

Printed in Canada by Friesens Corporation
Altona, Manitoba

For

Dr. Douglas Bocking

A great friend of the Thames River

Memories of a bygone village rise in the mist at Plover Mills.

FOREWORD

How many of us can name a river that has played an accompanying role in the shaping of our lives? In this country, there are probably quite a few people who grew up close to a body of water that was a constant companion through the years. Here and elsewhere, the great rivers of the world are celebrated in books, songs and motion pictures.

Canadian author Margaret Laurence, in her book "The Diviners", wrote about the river that wound its way through her life in the area around Lakefield, Ontario and was a silent witness to her triumphs and tragedies. American actor and director Robert Redford has given us the poetic, elegiac movie "A River Runs Through It", in which a father attempts to pass on to his children the fundamental principles of his life. While the movie is about fly-fishing, the activity merges with the central theme that the river, the fish and the whole world are God's gifts to use wisely.

As a boy growing up in southern Ontario, I was soon aware of the presence of the Thames and, as a resident of Stratford, its famous tributary, the Avon. In his collection of photographs, Richard Bain captures the evocative images of life along the Thames as it meanders through Canada's deep south. From its source near Tavistock, and its humble roots in the Ellice Swamp north of Stratford, the river rolls past the cities of Woodstock, London and Chatham and into Lake St. Clair at Lighthouse Cove. My own early path followed the river, as school chums and a girlfriend moved on to the University of Western Ontario and I found myself taking a career position in Windsor. The Thames and its tributaries were never far away.

This region has been home to people for over 11,000 years. While there are no descendants of the original inhabitants in the watershed, four First Nations communities, whose roots are from south of the border, live by the river between London and Chatham. Indeed, Americans have played other auspicious roles in the early history of the Thames. The river was one of the major theatres of the War of 1812. The great "Battle of the Thames" was fought near Chatham, claiming the life of the Shawnee Chief Tecumseh. Shortly thereafter, fugitive American slaves traveled the "Underground Railroad" to this area seeking freedom. Some of their descendants still reside in communities near Chatham.

You don't have to travel far to understand that the European settlement drive of the eighteenth century brought great numbers of British citizens to the banks of the Thames. The river is named, of course, for London, England's great river of legend and the proliferation of English and Scottish monikers on cities, towns, streets and schools demonstrates that the newcomers, who were braving a harsher climate in a strange land, wanted to bring with them a little bit of home in the surest way they could.

The folks in Stratford, who lived for a long time with their stretch of tributary dubbed the "Little Thames", eventually insisted on a name more befitting the classic style of their city which was named after William Shakespeare's birthplace of "Stratford upon Avon", England. The Canadian Avon was to become arguably more famous than its English parent when the hugely successful Stratford Shakespearean Festival rose on its banks in 1953.

Like so many other stories of burgeoning settlements across this country, the Thames district finds its modern-era beginnings in tales of the early settlers who came to the land near the river. The flats and banks along the water drew their incredible richness from the nutrients brought down from the great swamp to the north. In public school we would hear stories of the tall and sturdy Scot, Dr. William "Tiger" Dunlop, a Canada Company wilderness developer on a grand scale.

As Adelaide Leitch notes in her book "Floodtides of Fortune", on the history of Stratford, Dunlop was the first to record his visit to the north bank of the still unnamed Avon at the site of the future Stratford in the summer of 1827.

Canoeists are a frequent sight along the Thames. These modern day explorers
are travelling past River Valley Golf Club near St. Marys en route to the Thorndale Bridge.

He slogged along a stream "where raindrops sputtered on coffee-coloured water" and his heavy boots left marks in the soft river mud.

It was the end of the primeval era for the river and its future began to unfold. Pioneer farmers started clearing the land and the river was soon providing access for settlers, linking lake transport with road and later rail development.
Drive through the area today and you'll soon be impressed by the vast stretches of fertile farmland nestled here in the agricultural heartland of southwestern Ontario between Lakes Huron and Erie.

While the Thames was of practical importance in opening up the area, its real value to the people who live near its banks has always been the tranquil, picturesque background the river provides for so many everyday activities and family gatherings. Some of my earliest memories include images of picnics on the riverbanks while feeding the ducks and those famous swans on Sunday afternoons, family reunions with all the Robertsons spilling out into the parks for games and food, and long walks around the river on mellow spring and summer evenings with a young girl, of movie-star good looks, who was to become my wife. The same kinds of events bring families to the towns and cities along the river today.
Picture albums speak to the generations that have grown up around the Thames. They are filled with photographs of young mothers holding newborns at the beaches at Wildwood or Fanshawe, sweethearts in canoes, perhaps paddling near popular spots like Springbank Park in London, fathers dozing and grandmothers quietly reading or knitting.

Yes, this heritage river is the focus for many and varied activities, including cruising in pleasure craft from Chatham to Lighthouse Cove, and fishing for walleye, bass and Chinook salmon, which might also bring us into contact with fish and wildlife species rarely seen elsewhere in Canada such as the eastern spiny softshell turtle, queen snake, southern flying squirrel and Virginia opossum. A hike beside the Thames, next to the rich Carolinian forest, would probably find us picking out the trees of distinction that mark the area, such as sycamore, black walnut and hackberry.

Our walk could also bring us into contact with many species of wildflowers on the forest floor including such rarities as American ginseng, green dragon and wood poppy. Parts of the Thames watershed are also a birdwatcher's paradise with 157 species of birds breeding in the area. Those of us who grew up around the Thames also have one or two stories to tell about swimming, especially in the glory days of skinny-dipping. A favourite for swimmers of all ages was the spring-fed limestone quarry at St. Marys. A constable would show up occasionally, the same kind of fellow who would appear over the Romeo Street bridge in Stratford, and bellow out "suits on" at the white bottoms disappearing into the water. He never lingered for very long. Off he went... and off again would come the suits.

It's also possible to appreciate the Thames in winter, especially if you live in the snowbelt areas east of London. In the best of the real Canadian winters, it freezes solidly enough to provide a couple of good rinks for skating and pick-up hockey with tin cans and orange crates for goal posts. Snow-shoeing along its shores in winter can also be exhilarating, as long you carefully negotiate the softer swampy areas when spring approaches.

The Thames spans the seasons as it spans the generations of Canadians that have grown up near its banks. Through the years, its calm and constant presence has inspired the young who swore undying love to each other near its waters. Others paused to paint, perhaps the scenes around the river, perhaps designs from their own imaginings, helped along by the ambiance of the quiet currents. Still others, like a young Tom Patterson, would stroll around the river to contemplate big ideas and dream great dreams of a festival for the plays of William Shakespeare.

The Thames remains the link to our heritage in the reality of the present. It was there long before we arrived and will continue long after we've gone, as it wends its way through the lives of our children and grandchildren and the newcomers to Canada and to the region who choose to reside near its banks.

Lloyd Robertson

Fishing from lawn chairs on the natural limestone riverbed in St. Marys.

Enjoying a summer evening after dinner at the Riverview Restaurant
near Springbank Park in London.

I heard it once said that to know one's self, one must truly know from whence one comes. I believe this means not only our genealogical histories, but also the actual physical places we come from or live in. It is these physical places, embodying the breadth of unique and intertwined life and climates that shape and influence our tastes, our character, our dimensions, and our appreciations.

I believe, too, that we carry these influences with us in subliminal ways, just as bees scatter pollen, and in so doing, we contribute to the wheel of life that is always changing, fluctuating. It seems strange, then, that so often when we travel to far-off places, we look around us and say: "Oh, this is who these people were and are", but we so seldom think of taking account of our own locations, our own country, and how these have shaped the people we were and are.

To be a visitor, a spectator, is a wonderful thing, but to be of a place, a community, a landscape, is another, infinitely richer thing indeed. My hope is that this book of photos will stimulate our desire, be it as residents or visitors, to look upon the Thames with new eyes, to celebrate its richness and uniqueness, and in so doing, to understand one more aspect of who we are in the wheel of life.

Loreena McKennitt
Singer / Composer

The Tom Patterson Bridge is named after the founder of the
Stratford Festival of Canada. "The Little Thames," now known as the Avon River,
is one of the most picturesque tributaries in the watershed.

RIGHT: Spring melts away the winter snow at Ellice Swamp,
at the headwaters of Black Creek in Perth County.

Preparing for a Saturday morning exploring wildflowers
and water lilies at Pond Mills in London.

The Common Arrowhead *(Sagittaria latifolia)* emerges from the water in the Fish and Game Pond at Westminster Ponds.

Jewelweed or Spotted Touch-me-not *(Impatiens capensis)*
along Cedar Creek near Woodstock.

*The Thames River's health is affected by our daily habits.
It behoves all of us - government, industry, and citizens - to contribute to
keeping the waters clean and vibrant. When school children plant trees
and study water creatures they are part of the community working
together to conserve a healthy river and its inhabitants.*

Eleanor Hart
Volunteer
Oxford Children's Groundwater Festival

A dragonfly rests in London's Sifton Bog.

OVERLEAF: Wild mushrooms on a fallen tree at Westminster Ponds.

North of Mitchell near Brodhagen, the Thames flows before winter coats it with ice.

RIGHT: Winter's artistry along a snow drifted riverbank.

November mist along the river north of Thamesville.

LEFT: Early spring at the headwaters of the Middle Thames near Embro.

OVERLEAF: Elecampane (*Inula helenium*), brought to Canada by European settlers to treat coughs, can reach five feet in height.

A "Stratford Swan" on the Avon River is a familiar sight
for visitors and residents alike.

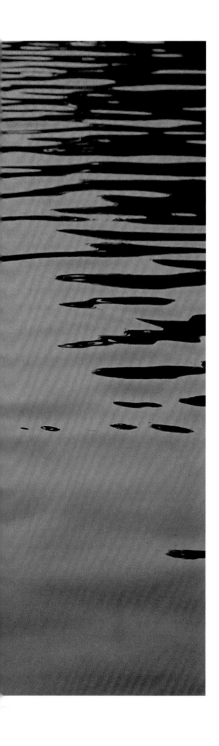

The Huron Street Bridge and the
Perth County Court House in Stratford.

Sun shafts glance off rippled waters toying with your imagination,
dappling shadows on riverbanks. The Avon River, heart of Stratford,
setting for romance and flights of fancy. What could be more perfect...
sunrise to sunrise, summer to summer, the river draws you
to its heart as it flows through town and joins
with the Thames like a little brother.

Steve Rae
President / General Manager
CJCS / MIX-FM

This Chaisson semi dory, tethered along Medway Creek,
waits patiently for its skipper.

LEFT: Watching the leader race towards the finish line
at the Rotary Dragon Boat Festival, St. Marys.

Along the river near Kilworth, icicles have formed on a fallen tree.

Winter mist rises from the river in St. Marys.

OVERLEAF: Near Thorndale, the river valley welcomes a new day.

Enjoying the activities at the Stonetown Heritage Festival in St. Marys,
held each summer on the second weekend in July.

PREVIOUS PAGE: "After the Storm", sailboats return to the water at Wildwood Lake.

*The Thames River flows, a fundamental theme,
through the history of this part of Ontario.
Our settlements grew along the banks of the Thames
and its tributaries. Its power drove the early mills
that made settlement possible.
The waterway was a lifeline for isolated
pioneers and its beauty lifted their spirits.*

*This book of photographs celebrates
the Thames and its rich heritage.*

Mary A. Smith
Curator, St. Marys Museum

Exploring the river on the limestone shelf
at the base of "Little Falls" in St. Marys.

A morning walk around Pond Mills in London uncovers undisturbed natural beauty.

Rowers from the University of Western Ontario practice on Fanshawe Lake.

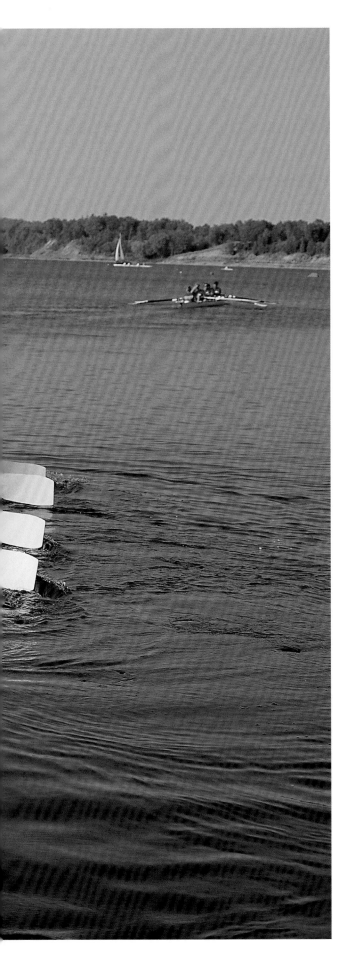

The Thames and Fanshawe Lake are under-utilized gems. My favourite time is the morning.... It is always calm and the sunrise can be spectacular. My highlight was observing the likes of Silken Laumann, Derek Porter, Marnie McBean and Kathleen Heddle (all Olympic medallists) rowing at peak speed across still waters. Other favourite moments have been spotting a diverse variety of birds and animals including Beavers, albino Mink, Great Blue Herons, Bald Eagles, Turkey Vultures and deer in a tranquil environment.

Al Morrow
Olympic Women's Rowing Coach

The crew carries its rowing scull down
to the water at Fanshawe Lake.

ABOVE: An aquatic biologist checks and releases an Eastern Spiny Softshell turtle near Delaware.

Along the sandy river bottom across from Springbank Park, a raccoon has left evidence of its visit.

LEFT: The old grist mill at Harrington Pond is all that remains of a bygone era.

The Thamesville Town Hall, built in 1911,
is home to the Chatham Kent Branch Library,
the Thamesville Old Town Hall Museum and Resource Centre
and the Chatham Kent Police Department.

The Oxford County Court House, built in 1891-1893,
is typical of many of the public buildings that were
constructed in the towns and cities along the Thames.

OVERLEAF: Captain John Harris built London's oldest residence, Eldon House, in 1834.
It overlooks Harris Park near the Forks of the Thames.

What look like miniature trucks can be seen at the base
of the quarry at the Lafarge Plant near Woodstock.

A mine truck loads lime from the load out bin at Carmeuse Lime near Beachville.

Nature has endowed the communities along the Thames River with an abundance of limestone. Materials that shape our roads, houses, churches, schools, hospitals and bridges are but a few of the products that are produced from the landscape surrounding the river. In return, we are always seeking new ways to protect and promote nature's precious gifts.

Christine Iddins
Lafarge Canada Inc.
Woodstock Plant

Students learn how maple syrup is made at the Fanshawe Sugar Bush.
Tours hosted by the Kinsmen Club of Greater London take place each spring.

A lone swan makes an unexpected appearance on Cedar Creek near Woodstock.

Even in the beginning there was art at the forks of the Thames. Indians had drawn figures
in charcoal and vermilion on the trunks of the trees. In 1807, the well known artist George Heriot
(1766-1844) wrote "on the east side of the forks…about 40 feet above the water
there is a natural plain…giving the appearance of a beautiful park."
Today, on the east side of the forks, we enjoy Ivey and Harris Parks and the Peace Garden,
with the recent addition of a water park of stonework and fountains.
On the crest of the bluff, crowning the Forks of the Thames, art and history continue
to intermingle in Eldon House, Museum London and the Old Court House.

Nancy Geddes Poole
Retired Executive Director
London Regional Art & Historical Museum

A great way to cool down on a summer day is at the Ivey Park Spray Pad,
situated at the Forks of the Thames in London.

The Royal Scots re-enact the Battle of Longwoods, which took place
along the Thames River on March 4th, 1814.

For the past ten thousand years, the Thames has been an important yet silent witness to the comings and goings of mankind and nature. These stories are the food of the living historian and this wonderful river serves up a bountiful buffet. It represents the richest source of living history activities in Southwestern Ontario. You can experience the Longwoods Heritage weekend in May, Fairfield Comes Alive in September and the Chatham Heritage Weekend in October. Our heritage river Thames is rich in historical fare.

Glenn Stott
Local Historian

The London Museum of Archaeology, located along Medway Creek,
is the site of Canada's only ongoing public excavation
of a fifteenth-century Native village.

RIGHT: The Moravian Village of Fairfield was one of the
first settlements in Upper Canada, established in 1792.
History comes alive each Labour Day weekend with
re-enactments and pioneer activities at the Fairfield Museum.

An abandoned service station found on Longwoods Road (Highway #2).
Today, with most of the traffic using Highway 401,
sights like this along the "old river route" are common.

LEFT: Experience the sights and sounds of life in the 1800's
at Fanshawe Pioneer Village in London.

A quiet morning on Fanshawe Lake contrasts
with the Victoria Day fireworks that illuminate the same waters each year.

Some early morning fishing enthusiasts get ready for a big catch at Fanshawe Lake.

Evening along the river in Springbank Park.

A cyclist enjoys an evening ride through Greenway Park
along the Thames Valley Parkway in London.

Feeding the geese in Springbank Park, London.

Camping on Labour Day weekend, Fanshawe Conservation Area.

Mallards gather together on the riverbank near Woodstock, before the fog lifts.

Along Longwoods Road near Thamesville stands
a monument to Tecumseh, who was killed near here in the
Battle of the Thames, October 1813. With him died the
Native people's hope for an independent nation.

*For hundreds of years, the Thames River and the peoples of First Nations
have lived in harmony. Each season is cause for celebration.
We must remember that we have not inherited this wonderful resource
from our parents; rather we have only borrowed it
from our children and grandchildren.*

Chief Thomas
Munsee Delaware

Children of Munsee Delaware perform a traditional dance near the river.

Evening by the Avon River.

Annual flower plantings add spring colour to the river bank.

The Thames River, particularly
the lower portion, is situated
in the southern part of Ontario known
as the Carolinian Canada Zone, which
ensures an early and warm growing season.
The proximity of the Great Lakes modifies
the temperature and humidity and
ensures a climatic advantage over
most of the Province. This combined
with extensive dyking and drainage
works, provides fertile farmland.

The river was crucial in the
development of the area as it provided
a "highway" for the import and export
of goods, a supply of food
and a conduit to other major
settlements located along
the river and the Great Lakes.

The history of the Thames River
region provides a legacy of significant
cultural and recreational opportunities.
Many examples of these are clearly evident
as one travels the Thames River region.

Jerry Campbell
General Manager
Lower Thames Valley
Conservation Authority

The Third Street Bridge is an ideal vantage point for Chatham Parks
and Recreation employees to help the boats navigate
their way to the municipal docks.

LEFT: Pleasure craft frequently make the river passage
from Lighthouse Cove on Lake St. Clair to visit the City of Chatham.

Young naturalists looking for crayfish along Medway Creek in London.

Previous Page: A natural bouquet along the Thames in the Village of Dorchester.

Autumn colour on the riverbank near Wardsville.

An aerial view of the Forks and Museum London.

*Like its more famous namesake, the Thames
is a river that helps define the people and places
of Southwestern Ontario. From the streams that are
its source, to the dams that control its fury-
from its famous 'fork' that became its largest
settlement, to the lighthouse at Lake St. Clair,
the Thames is a thread sewing together communities
large and small. Richard's photographs capture
the river's light, reflections and soul.*

Gord Harris
News Director
Corus Entertainment London

Watching the ducks in early November at Harris Park.

A spirited kayak adventurer finds some
"white water" south of St. Marys.

Day-dreaming about a bird's eye view of the river at the London Canoe Club.

Playing in the sand
at Pittock Conservation Area.

Taking a rest while cycling around Pittock Lake in Woodstock.

Tending to one of the many beautiful flower gardens along the Avon River.

The Arva Flour Mill, built in 1819 along Medway Creek,
is one of the oldest active flour mills in North America.

Bindweed (*Convolvulus sp.*) twines around other plant stems to reach the sunlight.

This former grist and sawmill was constructed in 1845 by John Finkle
on the east side of the Middle Thames River in Thamesford.

Trying to spot goldfish in a backyard garden west of Thamesville.

Getting the dinghy rigged for her inaugural sail
at Lighthouse Cove.

*For centuries, the Thames River has been
a "blessing beyond measuring" to those who have settled
on its banks and in its watershed. It was "civilization's first
highway" into a resource-rich area, and has since provided
the water for everything from shipbuilding to farming.
We should all give thanks for this quiet stream
that has shaped our lives in so many ways.*

Win Miller
Author / Historian

The late winter sun starts to open the river alongside Ormonde Horse Farm in Delaware.

In 1875, Blackfriars Bridge was the first iron bridge to span the Thames.
It linked the former village of Petersville to the Forest City.
This bridge is believed to be the oldest wrought iron bridge
still used by motor vehicles in North America.

Overleaf: An early November snowfall coats the trees and this secluded
foot bridge in the Medway Valley behind Huron College.

Returning home from classes during a January snowstorm on the campus
of the University of Western Ontario.

Ducks taking warmth from the
open water alongside Gibbons Park.

OVERLEAF: Pampas grass illuminated by an autumn sun along the river in Mitchell.

Enjoying lunch overlooking the river
at Michael's On The Thames in London.

RIGHT: The sun rising over downtown,
as the river winds its way through London.

Shopping along King Street in Chatham.

Farmers near Tilbury take advantage
of the long growing season to
produce a variety of fruits and vegetables.

Near the end of the Thames River's journey at Lighthouse Cove,
sailors have a sheltered harbour from the waters of Lake St. Clair.

The Stratford Festival of Canada attracts patrons from around the world.
The Festival Theatre is located along the "Little Thames" in Stratford.

*Once known as the "Little Thames", Stratford's Avon River is surrounded
by some of the most beautiful parkland in Southwestern Ontario.
It was here that the Stratford Festival first pitched its tent in 1953, and it is here that
the Festival Theatre still stands. That parkland – which 50 years earlier narrowly
escaped being developed into a locomotive works – has played a crucial role
in the Festival's success ever since. Without so idyllically gorgeous a setting,
the Festival dream might never have taken hold, and we would have been denied
the decades of inspiration and achievement that have flowed from this tributary
of the Thames to all of Canada and beyond.*

Antoni Cimolino
Executive Director, Stratford Festival of Canada

PREVIOUS PAGE: Morning fog starts to lift revealing Harrington Pond.

Black-eyed Susan (*Rudbeckia sp.*) along
the river near the Town of Ingersoll.

John Graves Simcoe, Governor of Upper Canada, knew that he had found a special
place when he arrived at the Forks of the Thames over two hundred years ago.
The community that grew from this site on the Thames has become a wonderful place
where families live and businesses prosper. The river, with its beautiful parks, trails and
year round activities, brings great joy and pleasure to our residents and is often a highlight
for visitors, including those we serve who are considering
locating a business here. The Thames is truly the heart of this great city.

John Kime
President & CEO, London Economic Development Corporation

The North Branch of the Thames River, hidden by autumn foliage,
enhances Western's beautiful campus.

Blue Vervain (*Verbena hastata*) can be spotted
in wet areas along the Thames.

Looking out across the river near Thorndale provides a tranquil view of the river valley.

Spending some quiet time
on the shore of Pittock Lake.

*It takes only a moment to paddle into another world.
That's what happens when you paddle the Thames River.
Skimming the calm waters behind Springbank Dam or riding
one of her standing waves in your canoe or kayak,
the Thames is a magical place right in our back yard.
Take a paddle in the twilight of a summer evening
and you will see what I mean.*

Colin Neal
President, London Canoe Club

Members of the London Canoe Club
gather after an evening on the water.

Light has shone from this spot at Lighthouse Cove to guide mariners since 1790. The original structure burned to the ground during the War of 1812.
The lower portion of the present lighthouse was constructed in 1818 and then extended to its present height in 1867.

At the end of her journey, the Thames River quietly flows into
Lake St. Clair at Lighthouse Cove, but hundreds of miles of memories
spanning thousands of years remain.

ACKNOWLEDGEMENTS

*Many residents of the Thames watershed share something in common.
They have only seen the river as they cross over its bridges going about their daily routine.
It is my hope that this collection of text and photographs tells a story of the wonderful
natural resource that we all share.*

*Countless individuals over numerous years have contributed to the vitality of the Thames.
This book is dedicated to Dr. Douglas Bocking, a great friend of the river.
His determination was instrumental in the Thames receiving the designation
of a Canadian Heritage River, a great inheritance for future generations.*

*Having one of Canada's most celebrated citizens and broadcasters, Lloyd Robertson,
agree to write the foreword was a highlight of this project. His personal reflections brought back
similar memories for me, as I'm sure they will for some of you. I am amazed at the generous
spirit of people who unselfishly dedicate valuable time to a cause in which they believe.
I would also like to thank Amber Nasrulla from CTV, who spent significant time managing
the foreword process.*

*Invaluable on this project was the guidance of Don Pearson from the Upper Thames River
Conservation Authority, as well as Jerry Campbell from the Lower Thames Valley Conservation Authority.
Their respective staffs were most helpful, but particular thanks go to Bonnie Carey, Brenda Gallagher,
Scott Gillingwater, Eleanor Heagy, Teresa Hollingsworth, and Cathy Quinlan.*

*I was honoured to have a special group of citizens who share a love of this river contribute
reflective quotes for the book. Thanks to Antoni Cimolino, Gord Harris, Eleanor Hart, Christine Iddins,
John Kime, Loreena McKennitt, Win Miller, Al Morrow, Colin Neal, Nancy Geddes Poole,
Steve Rae, Mary A. Smith, Glenn Stott, David Suzuki and Chief Roger Thomas for their insight.*

*Thanks to James Cowie and Kieran Wallace from Stan C. Reade for their generous support,
and Steve and Carol Grimes, Sheila Tofflemire, Pauline Raulston and Gloria McGinn-McTeer
for their advice and assistance. There are many others, too numerous to mention, who assisted
in this project. I thank each of you for your help.*

*It is always amazing how a designer can take a group of transparencies and produce a finished work.
Thanks to Brian Williams & Associates for their patience, and accommodating all the changes
that a photographer can throw their way. Thanks also to Tom Klassen from Friesens Book Division,
who was instrumental in the production.*

*I extend heartfelt thanks to my wife, Joan, and our children, Daniel, Caroline, Jordan and Brett.
Each of you in your own way has been tremendously supportive. I enjoyed all of our walks,
talks and time spent exploring different places along the river.*

*I hope that these photographs remind us all that we have a treasure in the Thames River.
Let us continue to protect it from harm, and enjoy all that it quietly gives us back.*

Richard Bain